DIVERTING THE SEA

EMILY WILLS

DIVERTING
THE SEA

Simon and Rachel,

With thanks for all your
creative support on 2nd July!

Love,
        Emily
                2·7·00

ACKNOWLEDGEMENTS

Acknowledgements are due to the editors of the following magazines, who first published some of these poems: *Borderlines*, *Envoi*, *The Frogmore Papers*, *Iota*, *Ore*, *The Poet's Voice*, *The Rialto*, *Rustic Rub*, *Seam*, *Smiths Knoll*, *Staple*.

First published in 2000 by

ᴛʜᴇRIALTO

PO Box 309, Aylsham, Norwich NR11 6LN

© Emily Wills

ISBN 0-9527444-2-2

The publisher acknowledges financial assistance from the Esmee Fairbairn Charitable Trust and the Eastern Arts Board

The Rialto is a Registered Charity No. 297553

Printed by Printing Services (Norwich) Ltd.

For Damian, Thomas Khwima, Elspeth and Lydia

CONTENTS

Five a.m.	9
Before	10
Gestation	11
Displacement	12
Diverting the Sea	13
Fifteen Cubits Deep	14
The Shadow Stone	15
The Willow House	16
My Friend Jane	17,18
The Cage	19
The White Step	20
At a Distance	21
Revisiting the Larches	22
Painswick Church, October	23
The Whiteness of Afternoon	24
Arctic Explorer	25,26
African Sisters	27
African Healer	28
Batik	29
The Box	30
Christmas Eve, Malawi	31
New Year	32
Chynoweth Garden	33
The Raspberry Net	34
Blind Lane	35
The Musician and the Blind Girl	36
The Weigh-in	37
Hilda	38,39
Prefabs	40,41
Stroke	42,43
Grandmother's Sewing Machine	44
The Couple	45
Annie	46

Waiting   47
Loft Conversion   48
On Wearing White (or Purple)   49,50
Variations on the Themes of Today   51,52
Lullaby of the All Night Superstore   53,54
Fully Automated Image Recognition Systems   55
The Smell of Oranges Reminds Her   56
Chinese Postcard: Three Pools Mirroring the Moon 57
British Rail Announcement   58,59
Chrysalis   60
French Plait   61
After the Children Left   62,63
Amnesty   64
Collage   65
Red Primroses   66
Side Effects   67
Say It With Flowers   68
The Soloist   69,70
Narcissi   71
Spring Tide   72,73
Brick Wall   74
Heartache   75
A Kind of Immortality   76
The Shoemaker Knows   77
Requiem for Sideboard and Continuo   78
The Apple Tree   79
Retrospective   80,81

FIVE A.M.

For her it is a switch on
sudden into how singing was
before that first morning,
eggshell-shattering, saw light.

While I, heavy
trawling below waves for dark
dreams, a deep mesh of weeds – see
shining the barb of her;
I always bite.

Hauled in
by her cry so fine tuned; dreams
splinter like blown glass, gasp
and fin the stranger air
drop back, resisting –

      only touch her
warm from the egg, so here
so all herself
so almost mine.

BEFORE

Was I there?

your absence empty as the mould
waiting on clay

Where was I?

you were the leaf that fell
shouting yellow at my feet
demanding pocketspace

you were the seed that grew
among disappointing sunflowers
blazing into autumn shocking
the sodden soil with brightness

like the dream survived daylight the echo
of a tune which is lost in its singing
you were wave pattern wind ripple
blown into sand over the vast beach
forcing bared feet to run in the salt wind
until the breath struggled with your
first gasp

you waited distant as star time
where light follows its end where each
eclipse is predicted and terrible
and shooting stars in perfect
random pattern firework the sky

> until
the moon cracked you
my wishing star sparking
hot scorching belief
burning to know

GESTATION

It's a coming together
of sounds to make a language
unheard, unspoken

it's a rhythm that sounds
before hearing or words,
a heart that beats
from the 25th day

it's a cuckoo's egg, this poem
whether given, or found
in that dark space
on this white page

it's a soft-shelled nut, a form
before meaning, a question-mark
of a strung bead spine

it's a metaphor, unrhymed,
a gender it won't disclose,
a tick-tock quickening, free verse
confined to two dimensioned space

and all you hear
is the black/white ultra sound
of lines that scan all ways, or none,
and all you ask
is what it means.

It takes three slowed-down seasons
to grow a poem, which even then
will not let on
how it will read
in five years' time, how translate
in fifty.

DISPLACEMENT

This the new substance
      surrounded
she names it   claims it hers
dipping and pouring
        plays endless
patient rhythms of slow rain fall.

Look
       this shape transforms
flat   rope-like   solid
shattering
      her hand
a fat pink sea-anemone searches
hungrily questions this confined sea

knows it open to hold her
closer than comforting   closer
than speaking
      but with dry
touch of words   will water
hold her still?

DIVERTING THE SEA

Trying to hold summer
I attempt photography
shiny smiles in rows, with corners
cut, no rain, no rasping sand;
I'm not the only one.

From dripping shrubbery he gathers petals
with cheeks creased brown
distils their juice with heavy spoon
sniffs perfume, tastes libation
      See
      it is pink as roses!

With small spade, huge faith
he is diverting the sea
dreams all night of his silting pools
slow dark stalactites growing
in limestone years of his mind
deep under inevitable tide.

By morning he flies like a flame
his kite straining past grey
handshake of wind
slipping through fingers of cloud

trying to hold on.

FIFTEEN CUBITS DEEP

Rain; not substance, but force
strikes bloated soil, blurring
days and nights like a crude lens.

Thrummed by this torrent, dark leaves
vibrate with shivering arpeggios,
resonate in drowned trees
praying their olive hands
to ash of evening birds.

Loitering like wet leaves
heaped by railings, we're pulled away
bent blind to a green wind,
the clutch of scarves, hands. Shut doors
making no boundary now
between rain, cloud, river.

Listen; the moon's voice calls
your name, as rain tears down
night cliffs of cloud, bearing you
over quick rising waters
past bent rim of refracted sky.

THE SHADOW STONE

Each night he waits,
the shadow-man, framed
in yellow square of light
crouched shoulder-bent, grey hands
clutching grey stone.

If you lie taut, rooting your eyes
on his hooded face, not blinking
he shivers as pale curtains blow
watching, taking aim.

If your eyelids slip
from damp hands netted with sleep,
he will sling that stone
in a hot white arc of ending

and in the morning they will find
only the small lost left of you
faded like the remnant of a dream.

Now in your nightlight sleep
I visit you, small girl
coiled in your nestbox warmth
close curtains, arrange shadows –
you stir and mutter under mine.

THE WILLOW HOUSE

Inside cupped palm of afternoon
warm as breath, cut grass exhales
slow growling spin of dandelions.

We are planting a house;
willow sticks straight and bald
corn-circling new grass.

As they grow, he will weave stems
dome-like above him
make tented viridian shade

shutting out sky. Now he shears
carefully between, searching for buds
on cutting edge of dreams, forgets

when they have grown, his wanting
will have branched beyond leaf boundaries,
stooped camouflage, into shrunken garden

remorseless light. Now he hides
where imagined doorways grow; already
he's learned the power of walls –

When people throw grass, there might be
stones as well. His sister chains
fat wrists with daisies, hurls new-cut
blown storm of splintered green.

MY FRIEND JANE

When I was small I had a friend called Jane
with hair spun gold and skin of porcelain.
You had to love her and you had to do
whatever she said –
she'd chosen you.

Say you did it
Black scrawl on the desk.
Say mine's best.
You'll drop the ball you always do.
Who's your best friend?
Pink doll nails meet in your arm
but cry out and you're done for.
Tell tale cut out your tongue
And anyway its lies.

Turn your back and count a hundred.
If you don't she'll scream and scream
and splinter sharp inside you.
You'd be tangled up forever
by that fine fair hair;
you'd be branded by the shame
because you didn't dare.
So touch her soft skin gently
never let her cry.

A hundred is for ever, too;
It's all gone quiet.
Carefully you look behind
but the playground is empty
and you're stupid and alone
with mocking laughter at your back;
and not a chance of telling.

Some years later I saw her again,
her face lined, now, like old porcelain.
Although I'd loved her, done what she said,
she was alone this time, not as tall
as I remembered, tasting again the dread
of her pale hair, of dropping the ball.

THE CAGE

You are so strong, kicking down
daffodils, throwing bruised stems
back in their faces.

We know the story: mothers,
stepmothers, smoothing their soft bodies
searching for definition,

leading you into this forest
marking the path with bread, saying
you're a good girl

and leaving you there.
Witches feed you sugar-lies, crumbs
marking the path all gone

no way back. The snake
bites into dripping fruit
splits skin, emerges
dazzling.

Obediently, you cast off
layer after layer of flesh, searching
where mind should be.

So small now, caged
in a shrunken fairytale
too weak to turn the page.

THE WHITE STEP

She remembers; bent slow with cold
sweeping smooth the yawn
of the cave, careful twigs
hissing like damp fire.

In chilly suburbs, she scrubbed
white doorsteps of their greyish light
rubbed out their evidence
waited another day's footprints.

Always, she thinks, the mother sweeps
the girl-child copies, the grandmother
keeps still stern watch. So generations
erase their history.

Today she has left them behind.

She holds layers of time like dust
soft on her hands, creates perfect symmetry
of perfect empty room, colour-matched
comfortless.

      Yet still obeys
past mothers at her arm, wipes out
her story before she writes it,
sweeps words, flowers, footsteps;

the white step waits for hers.

AT A DISTANCE

Arriving early, I let myself in.

Find you not yet back; the house,
tense bubble of light and shade,
paused between words. Empty vases
reflect in polished table, your diary
announces my coming. A shopping list
recites itself to eyeless spectacles
watching my every move.

You came, of course, and the house
breathed again.

Shadowed behind the familiar, I see a time
when, arriving too late, I find this room
airless, spent; your silenced book
yawning, your diary spilling its tomorrows
pointlessly, without you.

While in the garden your stilled voice walks
heaping white azaleas with bloom.

REVISITING THE LARCHES

I remember them first planted,
then massed child-high
so that for years there was no way
to follow where old paths hinted

at something lost. Now trees meet cloud
let fall low branches, brown and sparse,
to leave this sedimented space
where children spin and hide.

I walk cool sea-bed of their falling
in greenish light. Penned
between branch and soil, a small wind
searches the far sky's calling.

There was a pond here, I remember
clotted with frogspawn, reflecting
bare sky. Now, ferns uncoil constricting
tentacles, tongues without number.

I am the larches, spilling
into the wind chill fear of falling

I am this space of meeting
between growing and parting

In me, the pond, shuttered and gone
like an eye closed under fall of pine

I am the small cold wind
caught in a sea-dream of land
once glimpsed, now left behind.

PAINSWICK CHURCH, OCTOBER

Sheltering, we found in the church
a rainbow place, among ghosts
of sunlight, ghosts of stone names,
dead wars. We found two ships;
one full sailed, afloat in air,
the other a bright ark formed
by small hands, sprawling
its two by two on rich green land.

Today is another harvest. Two by two
we have found dry land, cast seed, built ships,
sailed them to nowhere in our dreams,
then brought our children here
to church, to water. Now, stone font
bears stiffly its rainbow of fruit
and flowers. In its scooped bowl
the waters have gone down
very slowly. Above bent heads
the ship flies like a dove.

THE WHITENESS OF AFTERNOON

strips trees of sap, leaves grey
twigs rooting paler sky. Quietly
the children flicker, slowed
passive with cold I watch
their fragile flames. Snow

drizzles from sky hung limp
as greying net, defines us inside
silent observers of burial. Outside
ice breathes on shut black glass.

Snow purls, obliterating
circles of white wind
spiral, blinding
monotone.

Something will crack
under such white wastes
of silence; the mind
shattering its crazed shell

snow-laden. One branch
sudden under low stone sky
breaks
and is received.

ARCTIC EXPLORER

As a true sailor fears the sea,
he admits terror of snow;
that vast white page
on which he writes his journey.

There is no horizon
between snow and sky, nothing
to tell one blank sheet
from the next. Snow-blind, leafing
through sheaves of whiteness,
he loses sense of direction
sense of self. His waking dreams
his years, his people, spool
across the big white screen.

On a good day, he dares
to see like a vision the full stop
of arriving. On an ordinary day
he thinks paragraphs. There are days,
weeks when he closes down
on the next hundred steps,
the next word.

Asked why, he says he's searching
for what's inside his head – there must be
other ways: meditation,
the analyst's couch, psychedelics,
paper, ink.

Reaching the Pole, he finds
only another whiteness, his arrival
only the sum of terrible steps.
He pauses, a black comma,
in bookfuls of white
pure space. Below him,
ice, three miles deep; within him
the deeper knowing
that he is nothing at all.

But he will do it again, one step
one word after another, his tracks
stuttering behind him, temporary,
waiting the final revision.

AFRICAN SISTERS

Even before dawn they come
where each sunrise is new burning;
sweeping, renewing the earth still
cool in the waiting grey, until
dust lies smooth, tuned like a drum.

It is a woman's song; the broom
ploughing and harvesting dust
sweeps to rhythm of planting and rain.
The troubled moon turns, and sees again
crops that wither before they bloom.

Mothers, healers, dancers; here they sweep
mark out their time. Their space
balances too near the edge, where earth
betrayed of roots, begrudges birth
where water like a secret hides too deep.

And if they sometimes pause
questioning futility (for seeds fall,
petals drop and feet disturb this dust)
would they lose soil they hold in trust
as desert creeps through neglected floors?

Now is sudden dawn; the sun
which is again and now and burning,
wakens the children who barefoot the dust
scurry and patter it, redder than rust
their drumbeat and dancing only now begun.

AFRICAN HEALER

Mama Bamanta
centred in circular light
inside her warm earth walls
coiled round with dark, she holds
your healing, your despair.

Mama Bamanta
sings to red soil, to river
splitting through rock where dream
meets dream and breaks
drumming on the shore of mind.

Mama Bamanta
blesses with hands that know
blood, plough and crying child –
draws singing intertwined like rope
tight around your narrow soul.

Mama Bamanta, come
to this place of thin song
pallid dreams and wanting.
Come in your red robes
darkly, your golden lamp
fuming incense and oil.

Sing me
my spirit dances like smoke

Sound me
to beaten heart of drums

Bring me
flying to your flame
as insects sacrifice
white paper wings
and burn.

BATIK

Hard shadows slice where wax
and water meet, where trees
deflect maddening sky.
Among vermilions, ochres,
burnt siennas, you reach out,
simplified to black, and yet
I can't come close, can't feel
such orange burdening sun,
such purple hungers.

Above your song, this brittle blue
of waiting for rain has cracked
like a pot quick-cooled.
Touched by your hectic hands
pale soil fissures, blooms
preposterous flowers.

Watching you, framed
on my dull magnolia wall,
I'm wax; resisting, pallid,
reluctant to touch. One day
when I think you're not looking
I shall wear fruit, dance flowers,
even sing. On white canvas, wax
breaks, opens to rivers of colour
seeping, staying.

THE BOX

is woven of morning glory; blue
impermanence crumpling as day
scorches towards that sudden black
moonless din of cicadas.

Opens like an eye to see
maize cracking with drought
parched road a shiver of purple
jacaranda. Inside

two painted seeds, pierced
polished on frayed string, spelling
S'ing'anga's magic; "*So*
soft spot close so man child be

Brave as his name, Khwima,
one of us". My son, one new moon
strange to us, wears blue beads
huge on bony chicken chest.

Long ago. Now the boy runs
forgetting roots and naming. I
carry beads, like a lock of hair
skin-close. So when mind

crumples tangled memories
the box holds safe its secrets: blue
purple, darkness, drought –
and first cry.

CHRISTMAS EVE, MALAWI

Already, they have carried branches
laden with heat, decked green
with white wool, as if wounds
or flowers bloomed –

or snow. But when I ask, they say
the white wool is stars; bare branches
threaded with light tell their own story
of journeying, of giving birth.

They make ready the high, white bed
where the day's firstborn will receive
wise gifts – soap, oil, flour;
such riches kings would bring

if they came this far. We search
this bare black sky for rain,
for angels: there are only stars
white and hot as wool.

NEW YEAR

waits her call, tense, gilded
for procession. Christmas
loiters like a yawn, garish
green-rinsed, tinselled
with husks of regret
needles, thorns for burning.

Time blinks like a midnight bird
hinting at wisdom; reflecting
only another dark rotation
round sleeping child, each breath
snagged with pale echo of crying,
each pause already older

as last year gutters and spits, turns wax
to water, water to wine and drowns
drinking in its own reflection.

Outside, beyond this black wind cursing
under a sky new pierced with light
faithful they journey still

shadowing the star.

CHYNOWETH GARDEN

It was an unlikely conception;
this triangle of field, sliced
by white concrete wall,
a kitchen garden mulched
with broken history,
and a mineshaft
girdled with wire and waste.

Slowly he worked, whole days
whole years, shifting hollows of soil;
unwrapped waiting paths, freed stones
to footstep and grasp,
while sediment of lichen crusted
on measured progression of shade
across mown field, up greening wall.

Rooted in raw metals, plants grew
strange among gorse and heather.
Rhododendrons gleamed
rare as pallid moths in autumn,
like song in a deserted chapel;
then wilted suddenly to dust
as if by burning, and he
kneeling before, sweet voices
brimming in his ears.

The mine is safety-curtained, now,
with ivy, blackberry. Far below
a stream still tries
the riddle of corridors, echoes,
hammerings; searching still
for answering bloom of copper
for glint of tin and candle.

THE RASPBERRY NET

With fruit still green, and only poppies'
blown petals imitating fruit, he took the net
mended and knotted, like a fisherman
riding dreams and memories of the garden,
then draped another year the fragile canes.

Fruit came, and the tempted thrush; a choking
frenzy of feathers, like stunned moths
banging the light with dusty
flutterings, that primitive terror
of swooping bats too close at dusk.

To birds he was another tree, a rock,
saint in a stained glass garden. Slow
patient as soil he cut mesh
cradling fragile song in those thick hands
scored with thorns. And free

the thrush did not fly at once; shared with him
first forgiven breath. Kneeling
by ruined net and swollen fruit,
feeling its eggshell-warmth within his palm
he knew another garden.

BLIND LANE

ghosts to nowhere now, vestigial,
seeking the church blindly between
five hundred patient years of trees.

Hears between snoring traffic the ticking
time of elm, counting her rings
pencilled towards extinction.

Catkins expose their spring to frigid sky
elder ferments false promises. Dandelions
crushed by generations have footstepped

striped warnings where tarmac, beast
backed, crouches for speed. Old games
echo and rhyme, then and now

a ball bounces the dusk half-seen;
now and now loud metal screams
too fast, pale eyes dazzling

child and ball, cut down
with white curse of mayblossom
carried indoors. Tarmac shrugs.

Blindly the lane breaks
new buds, lights chestnut candles
reaching out green supplication of hands.

THE MUSICIAN AND THE BLIND GIRL

Pan-pipe and flute,
this music pierces her skin
like marram grass. She hears
grey downpour of his hands,
his spattering fingers, beating
the drum of her body. She knows
that he holds his small guitar
as if it were a child.

He blows high, green tremolos
from ocarinas, bubbles of notes
like drowning;
stops with quick fingers
the holes of her eyes
so she fills with sound.

He takes this brittle shell
to his lips like wine,
tells how he opened its spiralling,
long stopped cry
with fearful hands.

Now his breath coils
through opaque corridors,
as if something lived again
in this fragile helix.

Behind her stone stare
something breaks:
green waves into rhythmic light,
the shell howling for the sea.

THE WEIGH-IN

She waits her turn, smiling
not speaking. It is a small step
onto truthful scales, a small hope
of being found wanting. The answer
needles her puffball watery thighs
her cushioned heart snugged
tight in its thermal case.
She buttons her wide coat
over her thin smile.

They wonder why she comes
whisper – *if I were her – such legs –*
such lard – such bread – until one day
with apologetic Polish vowels,
she tells of Siberia, where for years
her mother boiled roots, bound
six children with taut hope
above the earth. *Sorry –*
she says – *now I not waste*
even half a slice – Thin smiles
have buttoned up their silences.

Blessed from the supermarket aisles
she finishes each night her last
white crust: each day finds
miracles of more.

HILDA

The place was all her own;
her backbreak chairs and shuffling
chessboard floors, the untamed
polisher no-one else could handle.
Between the trolley queues she'd strut
cheering the sick, hoovering
at full volume the complainers.

She loved her subjects;
pallid blue-checked nurses,
orderlies and clerks. Graciously
she sliced cake, ministered true
and clichéd comfortings, poured tea
with disinfectant hands.

Among the swell of transfers,
temporaries, Hilda alone
spelt permanence, continuity
of care: she knew her mops
and skirting boards, she knew
her place

until they started calculating
performance indicators,
throughput, cost —
forgot to count the cakes,
forgot her name — charted instead
for her a different unmapped
continent of floor each day.

But Hilda knew her place.
In charge.
Left for a factory job, for continuity
of nude pink chipolatas, the untamed
girl on the next machine

who pours her tea. Behind them,
trolleys full of best pork skinless
queue for hours
and not one complains.

PREFABS

Built to last twenty years,
like peace, they thought –
like marriage – fighter planes
and bombs were melted down
for roof and walls. Enduring,
they grow perennials, pink-bordered
wallpaper, carpets, trellis,
lawns. All night the blackout
sheltering rain gunfires
their corrugated silences.

Fifty years, and privet thick
as cottage walls. The lean-to blooms
dark multistories of tobacco tins,
his hoard, his smell. She loves
to pollinate the cucumber flowers,
those pale, summer openings,
with a soft brush,
tenderly.

Temporary as their stay,
their sudden leaving. Looking back,
they watch through masks of wire
and barb, machines, smoke,
sirens. They've seen it all
before, unblinking lidless
windows, rosy paper torn
open to rain, trodden poppies
littering unmown grass.

Return is permanent. Something new;
red brick, roof tiled, built to last,
like peace
like marriage.
Landscaped, and without a shed,
they sit, they sleep,
demolished by such insulated
guarantees, such fitted kitchenness,
such silent, silent rain.

STROKE

Earthed lightening
random, deep inside his skull;
the sound of hours; this change
he cannot name.

Half of his face
still smiles, and words
rear up translucent, tipped
with white spray of consonants
but will not, will not
break on the shore of speech.

Sometimes, not one syllable
patterns his furious calm,
though he scans flat horizons
for perfect lisping wave,
for dip and unison of oars.

He rehearses; breath, throat,
lips, like a swimmer, awkward
in unfamiliar style, desiring
that single, fluid movement:
it will not come.

Only one unformed word
lashes his mind, a coiled
rope of sound naming him
naming this —

and this: the nurses' quick
caressing hands, their wanted,
elsewhere eyes that see
only a line of pen or brush
at the close of biography
unfinished,
ended.

GRANDMOTHER'S SEWING MACHINE

was a Singer
inlaid with mother-of-pearl
heavy as falling

key scrapes
uneasy in the lock
opens her story.

Grandmother sings, threads meeting
parting, cutting a furrow
between white waves of cloth

sings octaves of gingham
hems to hand-me-downs, sides
to middle and make do

sings to the past when crowds
listened and she, tuned
like a harp, golden

quickening the wheel her
heartbeat, the piercing eye
too small to pass through

turns from the song
with fast running stitches
meeting, intertwined.

To ask for her regrets
is trespass;
turn the key

Grandmother was a singer
once, her voice
heavy with pearls
rising, falling.

THE COUPLE

They don't use these rooms much, now;
eat in the kitchen, their slippers slow
limping on newspaper-spread damp floor
the smell of milk and lino.

They don't use voices much;
save words for Sundays, for the man
who comes to do her feet, for rain
inevitable as a lifetime of washdays.

Their faces have set in folds, pale eyes
reflect blankly the weather, black-and-white
staring headlines, insistence of church bells,
the years' stiff haul of mornings.

They don't use hands as we do;
only for journeying from door to chair,
from chair to door, now they have TV,
deep freeze, and single beds.

Their time hangs, shapeless. Side by side
they sit greyly together on white
plastic garden chairs, while the aging sun
blesses their faces, voices, hands.

ANNIE

Shifting small pains uneasily
from limb to limb, she separates
each movement to a rosary of bone.

Sleep is a slow unravelling
of ninety years; dropped words
old faces ladder at her touch.
Woken to hollow dawn
by catfall of milk bottles,
she too lies waiting collection.

Sifting her dusty memories
like flour, she kneads
dry chaff of words:
past it, senile, geriatric,
old. She knocks them smooth –
they prove relentless.

Here, faces come too close, smile
white, false as dentures
yawning in her glass.
They strip her down
like paper, call her "*Annie –*
dear". One by one

she holds them to the light
sees through them all.

WAITING

White-faced, the clock broadens its smile
slants past the time you said;
my coffee cools to this tarnished ring
fingering uncertain future. Looking in

I see a road blackened with rain, pulsing
with blue reflections; a hand
stopping your leaking words,
the back door of your mind
left open, swinging in the wind.

So I am gentled away
to a brighter than daylight midnight place
to tea in windowless side-rooms
to a small bundle of clothes.

I hear the children's quotable grief
suffer vertigo on ladders, let fall
storms of documents, blow fuses
pay bank charges; open the door
to insurance salesmen, trick-or-treaters
Jehovah's Witnesses; produce
teenage delinquents, break down
on motorways when it is raining,
see my flexible friends swallowed up
by a black hole in the wall.

Outside, a car clears its throat
slams me shut as a guilty book.
Blue bells are steepling out in the dark
somewhere else the rain is falling.

LOFT CONVERSION

I've tried the innovative approach;
creative use of space, low-voltage
uplighters, reflective glass. I'm furnished,
as the catalogues say, with inspiration
with class. Still there's no room

with so much need for storage
in this cramped post modern mind.
My sleep converts to a pull-out
workstation, my underbed spaces stuffed
with outgrown poems.

All day I pace out heavy duty
smooth veneer; all night I lie
nesting my eggshell dream
of a still, small, place
between bricks and sky

an upper room
unfurnished, unready, cool wind
blowing on whitewashed stone.

ON WEARING WHITE (OR PURPLE)

Today I am having my colours done.
An investment, she calls it,
the expert in pots of gold.

"Very few" she says "can wear white
when alive: brides, possibly,
or babies, or those patiently
horizontal but breathing."

She deals fortunes of colour;
crimson, baby pink, yellow –
which anyway my mother said
I never should. Burgundy,
russet, brown leave me pale
not interesting.

Powder blue, sky, sea blue
navy and gabardine,
should never be seen
with green. "Not so"
she says, green-eyed
blue-lidded.

I hold breath, as she questions
her mirror, which answers
truthfully, that purple is out,
even when I am old
and black of tooth and heart
and learning to spit.

Her fire's white hot, ready
for the guy or girl who's dressed
in black numbers, off-white lies.
She moves through flame,
vermilion, carmine, charcoal,
ash. I am white with fear
and it does not suit me,

shedding clothes, and skin
and hair. "Very few" she says
"look good in fleshy tones
while they are still alive."

VARIATIONS ON THE THEMES OF TODAY

"Remains of World War I soldiers have been uncovered
during the construction of a new motorway. A young
Iraqi girl is being flown to Britain for lifesaving
treatment and scientists do not know why
the population of nightingales is decreasing."

The nightingales will fly from Iraq
over the newly-constructed motorway
and be buried with full military honours.

The military honours were unearthed
when a small Iraqi girl, for purely
political reasons, left her desirable habitat.

The population of small Iraqi girls
with leukaemia, is decreasing,
and they are not using the motorways.

New motorways are increasing:
a survey is needed to find out why the remains
of World War I soldiers are nevertheless
declining.

During excavation, they discovered nightingales
who are now to receive lifesaving treatment
for what may be political reasons.

Small Iraqi girls will be surveyed,
with full military honours, to find why
their remains are not using available habitats.

Recently, desirable surveys have decreased.
Is this a side-effect of leukaemia treatment
on motorway construction workers?

Scientists do not know why
motorways are lifesaving, or why small
Iraqi girls can sing like nightingales.

Our newsreader, surveying us –
for purely political reasons –
from the desirability of her habitat,
reports.

LULLABY OF THE ALL NIGHT SUPERSTORE

From pubs, clubs, three-piece
semis they come, quieted here
by chilled litany of yogurt possibilities –
set, firm, low fat, no bits,
thick, custard, greek, organic.
By checkout time, even the kids
lie stilled, scarlet, glistening
like shrink-wrapped meat
under my red-eyed laserbeam.

Hush little baby, don't say a word
Daddy used to think it quite absurd
to take you shopping at 3am;
now he's converted to one of Them.

Now taped and selling well –
"90 minutes in the midnight superstore"
guaranteed to make them sleep –
wire trolleys plucking shelves,
cymbal fall of tinned plum peeled,
soft-slippered metronome, percussion
snare of packaging. a dozen
contrapuntal checkout bleeps.

Behind frilled blinds, this generation
sleeps, networking putty brains
with shopping sounds, bulk-buy images:
puddings nine days past best-before,
patacakes, gingerbread houses, roast beef
or none, one potato chip
or four, ten fat-free sausages, fish
once biting and alive, and more
more labels to obey: try me,
drink me, need me, grow
so you don't recognise your life
without me. Sleep now, baby,
sleep.

Hush little baby, don't you cry
Mummy's taking you to buy, buy, buy
Under the dazzling neon sky
The superstore sings you a lullaby.

FULLY AUTOMATED IMAGE RECOGNITION SYSTEMS

are only five years off
the Sunday papers say. I'm one jump
ahead of my time: already, I have you
face mapped, the zeros
of your eyes ticking in the dark,
the one plus one
of your touching hands,
the stop start
pause
of your breathing.
And I've random accessed all
your megabytes of memory.

You can't delete it, now: I have
your face bar-coded, the creases
lateral to the eyes, the fully
automated frown. We're fibre-optic
linked, however you protest
with words like *liberty*,
like *choice*. I have you
in my laser beaming smile
and in this micro-camera's eye
your image, recognised
whatever your disguise.

You can't escape
from progress, may as well
admit it now:
your circuit's closed.

THE SMELL OF ORANGES REMINDS HER

of his close-up skin, pitted and thick
glistening, as if he too waited
in blue-dark crumple of paper
for her hand, for the bowl she carried
hungry for fruit.

There is a key to this
there is a chain. Can it be hers,
the black shut book, too full
of words and openings, layered
onion-tight with tears?

She remembers the lit focus of one flame
burning so slow that shadows flew
up the walls like sharp beaked birds
opening, cutting, breaking.

And she, cupped like a stolen apple
quieted on pillows of unbrushed floor
split like a small, smooth stone
in the grip of falling rock.

She remembers the smell of oranges
their blinding, stinging juice.

She knows now that those tears
peeled from cut release of onions
are a different fluid from those of weeping;
and the toy can never be as loud,
yellow, longed for, as the one
she hauls from her mind.

So, she will put them away;
book, key, chain, split stone
the chipped, spoiled toy. But still
the smell of oranges reminds her.

CHINESE POSTCARD:
THREE POOLS MIRRORING THE MOON

The moon, I recognise;
you have skimmed its white image
from the other side of the world.

The rest is beyond translation, this place
of blue-grey light, where you found,
between endings and openings, this
small white space to speak.

But I do not hear these pools,
their blue foreign tongues of water,
the gag of biting fish, the tense verbs
of black, bent fishermen.

Five barbed Chinese letters float
on grey water. In smaller space than yours
they have caught hills, water,
hauled three white faces of this far
flung moon from mirrored sky.

Overleaf, your words loop thinly,
approximate. I do not hear
your foreign watery tongues,
your tense hand. I think how beautifully
with one hooked brushstroke
you could have said it all.

BRITISH RAIL ANNOUNCEMENT

"Someone has lost two silver rings
in a small strawberry jam jar.
They may be collected from the buffet car."

She, too, sits cloistered in translucency
as if speed slicked these windows
to curved lenses, distorting
all fields and faces from Glasgow
to Penzance. Silver promises
chime again in her ears,
high-pitched, splintering.

My sweet, my strawberry
loveheart, let me eat you
whole, let me ring you round.

Rings now she turns, turns,
tight on knuckles rimmed like glass
while the lid of her mind snaps
shut at the same place each time.

She has tried to free their shine
under trains, in soil, in sickness
and in wealth, for as long
as a slow train stopping
at every station.

But now she is leaving.

Two rings wait in the aisle
of plastic cups, indifferent tea,
veiling her own impediments
to feast, or wake
or parting.

She goes quietly, at Dawlish
where track meets sudden
silver rim of sea, and curved
glass waves turn, turn
like vows
cast on shut and silent sand.

CHRYSALIS

Outside, pale wind has combed
leaf by yellowed leaf
into an irritable sky
turned stale, electric
charged with waiting.

Inside, you are transforming words
to flight, may emerge
nocturnal, fatally attracted to lights,
or sun-bound, searching purpler flowers.

I heard you say it's over –
but he still sees the creeping form
of what once was, fills in
the gaps with inky tears
wept from his camouflage eyes.

Ear to the wall, I'm listening
for dissolved silences,
I'm waiting
for the sound of redblue
ochred words, the damp
unfolding of wings.

FRENCH PLAIT

She rouses me too soon from tangled dreams,
then stands, small ghost, in barely woken light,
grey-faced, grey-limbed. Only her pale hair gleams

reminding me of ripened barley, bright
as our brief time together. Now I know
our storylines were bound too soon, too tight.

You said you could not wait to see her grow.
You gave your likeness as a gift and left.
Her hair was short then. It seems long ago.

I start to braid. Three strands take turn for weft
and warp and centre space. The rhythmic weave
binds strongly three as one; my hands are deft.

She is impatient, as you were, to leave.
Her sleek head tosses and resists demands:
something is lost that hands cannot retrieve.

She has your eyes and hair, she has my hands,
my dreams of holding three in one embrace.
We are divided now to separate strands,
while hair now longer, looser, hides her face.

AFTER THE CHILDREN LEFT

I found they had taken with them
all my words. *Take what you like*
I had said, of mugs, blankets,
biscuits, not thinking
to be stripped so silent. Days passed

the telephone rang, questioned,
stopped. I mopped spilt flowers,
spilt milk, washed gravel
stained howling knees, fresh tears
from sleeves. It was then I noticed

I could hear everything:
disagreements of forks and spoons
mugs chipping edges off each other,
the doorbell clearing its throat
tactfully, boots and shoes
battling for the doormat's damp pelt.

I could hear geraniums
wilting with embarrassment,
moss growing on stones, ivy
planning escape, snails
reciting the Beatitudes.

I have not slept or spoken since.
There is no room left for speech
jostling among the whirr
pause click rewind replay of
Nobody understands. Nobody
listens. I wish....You said
You always.....

They will return, one flowering
geranium flushed day, carrying
their own children. Muffled tight
with my words worn thin, they will offer
the gift of speech as if it were new
as if it were theirs. *Always you said,*
you wish, I listen.....
Nobody understands, nobody......

AMNESTY

Metal bars deform
his constant shadow in her bed.
His body, their dark strength
'Touched'
        – their word
skims syllables of torture
absolves them: hers retraces
burning speech of hands.

She writes. Not often. Words
ghost above the page, fragile
disobedient things, her faith
flickers and dulls. Perhaps one
white page reaches him there, shows

in bare rectangle of space
the grown child take the last
left place at table. Perhaps he hears
slow drumbeat of returning rain
eroding the proud hurt of leaving.

It was an improbable resurrection:

After, it should have been different –
                or the same
It was neither. Only an old man tamed
whose slow words limping drew
her reluctant hands
to scars stitched in his side.

COLLAGE

After the fire, we found

a tin cup, mouthed by gulping soot
a crumpled kettle, poured out, dry
glass bottles crazed tuneless with heat,

two coathangers, their thin shoulders
stiff with loss; one plastic shoe
deformed, the branded oil-lamp,

inside the small dark space
where his hand reached out, perhaps,
to steady its falling; and there

the sick, charred stench of meat.

Combing tangles of ashes
found last week's pay flaking
like dead skin, a wooden doll,

sugar baked into coal, black teaspoons,
coins, the clasp of a necklace, cloth
shuddering to dust as it met with air,

and, focusing on its melted heart
his camera, his proud skill
blinded by what it had seen.

I shall arrange these things:
spread cups, spoons, charred sweetness
on fragile cloth, make light,

retrieve patterns of metal, carved wood
from his camera's blank stare; background all
with thinned door gaping at sky

and with blunt charcoal, ashes
shade in spaces of our unknowing
under his black and reaching hand.

RED PRIMROSES

I watch the sky; there is snow forecast.
You say you suspected for some time.

I carry shopping, satchels, books.
You arrange words and probabilities.

I am far away. I tidy rooms. I sleep.
You remember the three days we spent
on the cheapest bus to Greece.

I buy flowers and watch them opening.
You wonder how to tell the children.

I am shut inside. It is March
and should not be snowing.
The flowers are too red, the wind too cold.

The children are tight buds filled with words.
You will not see them opening.

You are shut inside. You watch the sky.
I feel I have known this for all time.

You tidy rooms. You sleep. You are far away.
The snow is too red, the flowers too cold.

SIDE EFFECTS

Last year, stupified with hurt,
you laboured his huge paved skull
out into screaming air. Now
there is no pain, not yet —
only this growth, unquickening.

I pass on the news. People say
She was the one with the curls
I would have died for —
Silver threads embroider your shoulders.

Under the shower, my own hair
thinned by water, I have traced
pale eggshell curve of bone
as if it were yours;

imagined your scalp each day
more newborn. Now, you kneel
to your child, steadying
his first staggered steps. His grip
fists out fat handfuls of hair

delivers your naked skull
into the screaming air.

SAY IT WITH FLOWERS

I choose mixed bunch
in cellophane, hoping the red
if not the blue, white, purple know
what *It* could be. There's little room
in the box marked messages
and I can't wish you many happy
any more; 'though you've notched up –
Just – another year before you go.

The shopgirl translates from her menu
to suit all occasions, suggests
it would be more appropriate
at such a time
to leave out the lilies.

I'd forgotten they speak so loud.

Multitudes of lilies, discarded
from all our mixed bunches
waiting to have their say;
their blood-white calligraph
on damp earth, their dripping stems.

But you got there first; no flowers
please, but pink bloom of daughters
and tall-stemmed son. You left no room
in your box for messages, spared
even the lilies
their loss for words.

THE SOLOIST

It's over now: applause,
flowers, the deluge of notes
freed from taut strings,
leaving us filled with sounds
we cannot play.

In your spaces, you have allowed us:
black seated rows of earnestness
behind your scarlet silk. Brief unison; then
as the final theme transformed
monstrous under your living bow,
we let fall fallow hands
tuneless, listening.

You were unsure of your body,
its untried ranges, all of us
unrehearsed. But you knew
we were behind you,
in black neat rows, made small,
not knowing how our parts
would fit with yours
nor how you would leave them behind.

I sing your tunes
less often now, no longer sure
if all the notes are really yours, or if
I'm filling in your rests
with grace –
notes, slurring your staccato.

It's over now,
the score of your life reduced
to black on white. After the applause,
flowers; after the flowers
our untimed shuffling
into your left spaces.

NARCISSI

Evening locates each pale flame
huffed by wind. Somewhere beyond
this framed darkening, your name
scatters where it can't be found.

Planted hurriedly; before snow
snuffed silver-paper skins,
stiff with hoping that you'd know
a few more tapering springs.

Yellow, predictable; as flames
in uncertain light receive blown
petal fall, a slow, cold spring reclaims
that unlit hope as all your own.

Evening locates you somewhere
else; remote now, undefined
by obvious grass, this prayer
of early candles lit by wind.

SPRING TIDE

He's dusting her stories
from cluttered shelves,
plucking long-shed needles
from the soft pile of himself
wondering at the hurt.
It's a new year, clean slate,
spring tide that blows nobody
no good.

There are freak storms, ice-caps
melting, tornadoes in Sussex,
blackouts in Cornwall for days
and days. He's not surprised:
she always made her presence/
absence felt.

He's double-glazed and battened down,
he's changed the locks and changed
the bed. Cobwebs of her touch
still brush his face, in corners
he least expects: creased score
of the scrabble game
he almost won, her songs
he couldn't bear, her lists,
her unpaid bills, her half-read book,
a combful of lisping hair.

He catches this fallout rain
in whispering obese black bags,
prepares to bin this storm
and start again.
                      But then
unslept, the still-dark morning
finds him furtive, frantic
plundering an ill wind for all it brings:
brooches, lipsticks, scarves,
the anorak she always wore,
the lowtide calm of first meeting.

BRICK WALL

From all his windows it is there
blocking out sky; relentless
stepped pattern of cement
leading his eye upwards
to a loss already known.

It is a new wall, built quickly
like all the others, red and raw
as worked hands. Already he bears
the graze and gash of every brick.

In time, he knows, salt winds
will weather this grief,
slow ivy feel blindly into seams
easing them apart,
creeper will touch gently
with green spring hands.

They say it takes years.

Now, he cannot even imagine
dark ivy silvered with warmth
the laying on of hands. Now
he will watch slow days slide,
pause, thicken
like grey rain
patterning shut glass.

HEARTACHE

He could locate the pain
precisely; through barred gate
to red slow-silted stream
found he half-recognised the place

these hills lipped by low sun, a dream
of evening where he could create
from bruised seeping stain
ease, coolness, grace.

She can locate the pain
precisely; left chest, deep weight
of stone, like a scream
hurled into huge deserted space.

A KIND OF IMMORTALITY

From her clouded eyes
memories of sisters, brother
polished like worn silver
reflect reluctant brightness.

Sleepless, she salts down
their greying faces
into her closed glass dreams,

"His letters flew" she whispers
"airmail, from Africa
regular as prayers. I woke
to the creaking letterbox,
scrabbling dogs, his words
slit open with sharp knife

I saw again his face
last night, as near as yours,
as full of blood
as breathing."

Their images falter
tired of being kept alive
in the watery cave of her constant
remembrance.

Still she wakes to sallow dawn
yawning letterbox
spitting from toothless jaw words
lighter than breath
her old dog sniffing for letters
finds nothing but air

knife-edged,
shivering.

THE SHOEMAKER KNOWS

that the foot is an ugly thing
that his own peel onion-white and sour
that he is unemployable anywhere else,

knows he can make any foot dance
where a bad fit is a boot of thorns
and secretly, he would rather go barefoot.

He knows a pair is not identical
that his mistress wears pink nylon slippers,
he bears varicose veins from lifetimes of standing
and calluses at the corners of his smile;

knows this his life-walk, to touch
stripped posturings of rich men,
supermodels, kings, with healing hands
so they may forget him entirely.

He knows he is only one attempt
by the great cobbler in the sky
on a last that is worn and breaking;
that when the waxed hide of his body
is scuffed and sore, he will be replaced.

He pictures the Great Shoemaker trying
once more to achieve that vaulted arch,
that painless bearing, graceful stance,
thinking as he moulds and stitches:
this time, perhaps, the flawless fit,
the perfect, seamless heel
the blameless pair.

REQUIEM FOR SIDEBOARD
AND CONTINUO

When there is nothing worth hearing
on Radio 4, he silences lame scales
from our laborious instruments,
and performs, solo, the sideboard.

All stops and drawers pulled out
fortissimo, he silver flutes
pearl-handled knives into harmonics,
ornaments black, chromatic wood
in counterpoint. Doors bellow
lungfuls of mouldy breath
and old white china sings
to his touch like ivory.

His blunt, staccato fingers
transpose, invert,
resolve; his heavy feet
metronome the floor. Stiff hinges
sustain vibrato, and carvings
intone ground bass, repeat
al fine.....

Quieted and dusty now, the sideboard plays
diminished intervals, accidentals,
rests. Black gargoyles tongue
their brass rings silently, doors
are double-stopped and mute.

I imagine the headlines:
*World premiere, the long lost score
of a neglected master....*
and there, in the Albert Hall
our sideboard, polished
concert pitch, plays *Requiem
aeternam dona eis Domine.*

THE APPLE TREE

Each day, as bare bone winter
fingers of apple bark create
illusion of green, she watches
her own disobedient hands

arthritic as hawthorn bent
to prevailing wind; play dead
play winter, remembering

Grandmother, planting roses
stiff in metallic soil, lead paint
flakes on balding wartime velvet,
many small hands create a garden

where first pink bud shouts
from leaf to leaf and slow
ferns unroll for croquet

she is scattering seed:
weeping onions, cabbages
misting the windows of winter,
many winters before spring

white drifts of water-colour
blossoms flower on flower
obliterating green

where small girl chases
warm snow of petals; tries
to grasp dissolving sky
before they light on her

before time of falling
when brittle paints expose
grey garden. Interfering hands

push seeds from fingers
stiff with planting; offer food
platitudes, speak
too loud, too slow

face chair to blank window
white wall unfurling
white silk flowers

she always did love flowers
children, the colour white,
roses, apple blossoms

which never fall.

RETROSPECTIVE

1 In the beginning
   fingering bluegrey flint
   I saw shaped arrowhead wait
   my slow releasing fist.

   Crouched beside stubborn flames
   watched as raw clay, smoothed
   between drinking hands
   assumed curved grace of daughters.

   And I knew
   this would be handed on
   like fire.

2 There was huge presence
   trapped in callous stone.
   I, with hard chosen strength
   worked as if spell-bound
   daring to make bare.

   Scaffolded too close
   to heaven, heard muttering
   blasphemy!
   For God leapt from my brush
   stretching his painted hand
   touched me
   as if I were another Adam
   chased from this garden
   pursued by burning.

3 And after fire
   light
   infinite in variety
   on old stone, new harvest
   blown curves of sky,
   on forms no longer
   requiring definition,

   They stare
   cautiously,
   through smoked glass
   colour blind.

4 Light
   splitting like flint
   to blue and silver;
   sound vibrating sense
   long before listening.

   I painted leached sand
   marbled with fish-scales
   grey clouds' torn linings,
   quick shoals of rain.

   The salt wind chills
   keening through figures
   hunched, grimy, poor
   unfit for exhibition.

5 This branding flame
cannot be stilled
burns to renewal, release,
annihilation.

I construct galleries
of imprisoned sound, movement,
unformed questioning
where mind's eye
transforms like mercury
liquid   metal
poisonous   cure
or art?

The public
peering into ashes
peck
gorge
spit
and self-destruct.

For this
I have been searching
for this
I hand on
the flame.

Crouched child high
I move white pebbles, moss,
make ritual fragile
as veined leaf sealed
in ancient stone.

Selecting avocados
I cut oilpaint flesh
move seed
create at last
imprinted space.
Take.
Eat.

6 Older now, exploring distances,
I listen as rocks give way
to sand, where slow mind gullies
with low tide
watercolour wash of estuary.
See place baptised
to other medium; not clay
paint, words
but indrawn breath.

Born in Hampshire in 1958, I did most of my growing up in Cornwall. My father retired from teaching maths to create a garden, and my mother is an artist. School was memorable for the sea views from the bus, and for an inspiring English teacher who introduced me to contemporary poetry. I survived medical school at Bristol, and then trained in general practice in North Devon. My husband and I worked at a rural hospital in Malawi where we also researched health beliefs and the practices of traditional healers. Now living in Gloucestershire with three children, I am a part-time GP, very-full-time parent, and try to find a place in between for poetry.

I have always written notebooks, letters, and diaries, but there have been long gaps without poems. During times of exams, babies or melancholia I write very little and feel I have lost another sense. It has often taken years to shape an experience into something close to the just-right form of a poem. When writing goes well, I love the process: the play with words and sounds, and that intense concentration which eliminates other thoughts.

A poem often begins with a phrase or image, then develops into a story. Sometimes a landscape may hold the images which retrieve a memory, a person, or a powerful emotion. Other poems make up a diary, a sketchbook, by reminding all the senses that something was. In writing, I try to make sense of the stories I hear and experience, searching for a kind of healing through words and the spaces between them.

Emily Wills